MW00617046

AWAKENING THE MYSTIC IN YOU

Messages of Light from the Christian Mystics

Ramona Harris

Hamilton Books
A member of
The Rowman & Littlefield Publishing Group
Lanham · Boulder · New York · Toronto · Plymouth, UK

Copyright © 2010 by
Hamilton Books
4501 Forbes Boulevard
Suite 200
Lanham, Maryland 20706
Hamilton Books Acquisitions Department (301) 459-3366

Estover Road
Plymouth PL6 7PY
United Kingdom

Library of Congress Control Number: 2010935127
ISBN: 978-0-7618-5363-3 (paperback : alk. paper)
eISBN: 978-0-7618-5364-0

This book is dedicated
to the memory of my precious, joyful grandson,
Anthony,
who taught me the importance of
being in the present moment.

CONTENTS

Contents

Contents

PREFACE

"Awakening the mystic in you." Sounds intriguing, doesn't it? Do you dare to entertain such a thought? Let me explain how I discovered the wisdom of the Christian mystics; how their conveyed messages helped to awaken the mystic in me and can help awaken the mystic in you, too.

During the last few years, I have been exposed to quantum physics, new science and new age thought from current best-selling books, personal scholastic adventures, public television programs, Oprah, and new age friends searching for God outside the confines of a church building or a specific religion. These are people who are spiritual but not religious. As a co-owner of a small holistic gift store (which seemed more like a sanctuary than a store), I saw many people come through the doors searching for something to help them enhance their spirituality, self-esteem, or assist them in their quest to become more authentic in their personhood. Their spirituality came from a variety of faiths or traditions, be they religious, scientific, new-age, interplanetary or earth-based. My desire was to be open, inviting and able to converse in a nonjudgmental way with the customers as they poured through the shelves of books, cds, incense and the like. When I felt the gentle tugs on my soul as they shared their spiritual ways, it was helpful for me to stay grounded in my own belief system while keeping an open mind to theirs. Amidst all of this new science, new thought and new age, I too, continued the pursuit of deepening my spirituality. In this pursuit, I happened upon a hidden treasure of wisdom from an ancient age, a powerful elixir for the ails of humanity: the astute narratives of the Christian mystics. I believe their wisdom writings were meant to be shared not only with select Christian groups (monks and nuns) but also to be shared across the ages, with all seekers of wisdom and truth.

Even though I vigorously studied Catholicism long into my adult years, I was not exposed to the intriguing and inspiring Christian mystics until I was well into my forties. The first mystic I "met" was Julian of Norwich, a 14th century Catholic English woman whose spiritual visions amazed me. While on her deathbed, Julian received a series of visions from God she called, *Showings.* In the following days her health miraculously improved and she recorded her visions. Years later she wrote a second more detailed and insightful commentary about those visions. Julian's voice was quite different than those of the catechism teachers who taught me during my formative years. Her visions contained a *feminine* imagery of God. She dared to portray Christ as a loving, caring *mother.* Her views underscored a profound understanding of God's infinite mercy toward humanity. During her visions, Julian received God's assurance that "all will be well," even when she posed queries that confounded her about some Catholic Church teachings of the times. For example, in Chapter 32 of her book,

Showings, she asks God how "all will be well" when the Church teaches about sin and condemnation to hell for some sinners? It seemed quite bold of her to inscribe her accounts since in her day more than a few women were burned at the stake for professing views which differed from the Church, views which might smell of heresy. Nevertheless, Julian faithfully recorded the visions even though there could have been dire consequences from Church officials. I found Julian to be on the cutting edge of spirituality both then and now. As my knowledge grew about this great mystic, I developed an eagerness to learn more about other mystics and the deposit of treasure their works may offer.

While in graduate school, I read Harvey Egan's book, *An Anthology of Christian Mysticism.* His book was a watershed that furthered my understanding about mystics from early Christianity through the 21st century. I found that although many of the writings of the mystics were directed to an audience of monks or nuns in a monastery, their messages are applicable today to a wider audience. Their writings reflect the signs of the times (e.g. Crusades, inquisitions, black plague, heresies, mortifications, and institutional atrocities). Yet even with such upheaval surrounding them, they were amazingly masterful in their ability to speak of a deeply spiritual, unifying connection with God as a way to transform themselves and the world.

I realize as many Christian mystics as there are, each seems to have a slightly different approach in the way he or she interacts with the Divine. This variability lends itself to an appreciation that there are many pathways available to commune with God and no particular way is the only way or the best way.

Awakening the Mystic in You shares the insights of mystics whose expressions of love cross over the boundaries of creeds. It is primarily written for those who have some understanding of Christianity and its tenets. It may be of particular interest to spiritual seekers, spiritual directors, chaplains, lay and ordained ministers and others who choose to take a holy pause, delving into the mystery we call the Divine. It is not meant to promote rubrics or doctrine. Due to the nature of mysticism, the spirituality that comes forth from these mystics transcends religion as does this divine mystery we call God.

The majority of the mystics I have written about are either Catholic or Orthodox, due to my familiarity with them through my Catholic college education. The list of mystics in this book is not exhaustive. There are many other Christian mystics which I have not mentioned here. There are many mystics from other faiths and traditions that could be written about as well. Several of the mystics chosen for this book are considered by scholars to be classics in Western spirituality. However, I venture to say many of these mystics remain largely unknown to the average Catholic sitting in the pew and are likely unknown to those of other Christian denominations as well.

To introduce the reader to these particular mystics, a brief biography as well as personal reflections were formulated to complement each mystic's pearl of wisdom and to assist the reader in pondering the significance of the mystic's message. I acknowledge my interpretation of the mystics' writings is only one among many. There is also a *How to Use this Book* section which is a transformational tool designed to lead the reader to an insightful reflection of the mystics' words and to consider how these words may apply to one's daily life. The book is ordered in a topical manner. The reader can choose a topic of interest and be directed to a particular quotation related to that topic. Since there are 52 mystics disclosed here, a reader could make use of this book as a year-long reflective journal getting to know a different mystic each week.

It is my hope that those who read this book will be touched by the incredible joy revealed by the Christian mystics. While there are varying opinions about who might be defined as a Christian mystic, I believe we are all called to be mystics—to be fully present to God in our everyday lives and to be a beacon of God's light and love. This book has been written to help awaken the inner mystic who abides within each one of us.

ACKNOWLEDGMENTS

I am appreciative for the many people who took time to review my manuscript and offered suggestions to make it more reader-friendly: Joann Blaska, Ann McGuire, Marilyn Backland, Steve Ross of World Research Foundation, Laura Evnin, Gayle Thornton, Susan Kennedy, and Tom Broderick. A special thanks to Victoria Koulakjian, Assistant Editor, Production, Rowman and Littlefield Publishing Group, for her gracious professionalism in helping me format this book.

I thank my children, Cammie Harris, Shannon Harris and Erin Harris Standley for their absolute encouragement and support of this project. I am grateful to have such lovely daughters, and for their gift to me of grandchildren from whom I have learned many spiritual lessons

Many thanks to my spiritual director, Angela Garcia, for the hours of listening she dedicates to me; and for my personal spiritual direction formation at the Mercy Center, Burlingame, CA. I am grateful to my spiritual director supervision group members including my spiritual director supervisor, Julie Dent and Sister Sylvia Post for providing me with spiritual nourishment for my journey.

A special thanks to my soul sister, Sofie Pettygrove, who for years with a delightful, childlike honesty has shared her love of the Trinity, Mother Mary, the Saints and Angels with me. Thank you, Sofie, for sharing your lessons and experiences with me. You brought the realization of "expecting a miracle" to my everyday life.

I am grateful to my adoptive parents, Harry and Pearl Roll, for the personal sacrifices they underwent to put me at the center of their lives. I am especially grateful for the beautiful gifts of faith and extended family which they bestowed upon me. With that inheritance, I was inspired to pursue the development of my own spirituality and to embrace the divine mystery we call God.

Finally, I give honor to all those who have passed through my life and helped form me, in the light and the shadow, for I learn from both. I honor those who I have mentioned and not mentioned: biological parents, friends, relatives, teachers, and others; some names remembered, some names forgotten, and some names remain unknown. The list would probably encircle the globe many times. Thank you all.

INTRODUCTION

St. Iranaeus wrote, "The glory of God is the human person fully alive and the life of a human person is the vision of God." (Adversus Haereses 20:7) But do you ever feel disconnected with life, like you have lost your way? Have you ever felt as though you are moving through your day at such a rapid pace you hardly have time for yourself? Or, do you sometimes feel like you are slogging through life, working hard to make ends meet but just can't find the joy in it all? Wouldn't you rather live life to the fullest, be happy, find peace, be satisfied with yourself and those around you, even love yourself? If so, be prepared to begin your journey toward fulfillment of these desires as these Christian mystics help awaken the mystic in you.

Mysticism and mystics are not relegated to Native Americans, Buddhist monks, Vedic gurus, Confucius, Lao Tse or Sufism. Christianity also has its sages, wise men and women throughout the centuries, who spoke words from another time and place that sound strikingly similar to new age thought or new science. Their words lift the spirit yet are practical at the same time. Their words help us to center on God's loving presence, which they tell us, is with us at all times. The Christian mystics are liberators who break through religious walls as they expand upon the pages of Hebrew and Christian Scriptures. Their messages are like gems secreted in a cavern, and if one looks closely, one can discover a treasure-trove of extraordinary measure: messages of consolation, inspiration, motivation, love and light all which emanate from the God Source.

Christian mystics have encountered the Holy in varied ways, each with his or her own particular approach, each driven to a deeper, more intimate relationship with God. No matter how they felt drawn into this Mystery, the mystics ultimately responded by living their lives authentically and to the fullest extent. They were impelled to spiritual wisdom by an inner voice that seemed, paradoxically, to come from beyond their own three-dimensional beings.

Many of the Christian mystics were directed to write their stories, to our advantage. We are now able to tap into their sacred insight of oneness with the Holy. We can see and even relate to the pains and struggles they endured, both physically and emotionally, human like us in every way. We can see and identify with their pitfalls and watch their rising to heights that were thought unimaginable. These mystics have written with extraordinary candidness about their lives: their sufferings, their aloneness, their joys and ecstasies. These dualisms were inextricably intertwined. In the shadows or in the light, it was God who was their ultimate sustenance. In the mystics' writings we can sense their total communion with God, a unity that brought them to their completeness of being. They wrote frankly about being exposed to spiritual darkness, temptation and void, yet they also wrote with vigor about their yearnings to be in the warmth of the spiritual light and God's embrace. Their relationship with the Divine held out hope for them during difficult times. For them God was the light that illuminated their paths as they continued their walks of life, sometimes stumbling but always getting up again. It was Divine love which nourished and nurtured them along their way.

This book focuses on the "messages of light" found in the Christian mystics' writings. The word "light" is used here as an umbrella overarching faith, hope, and love. The mystics believed in a life force greater than themselves, who cares for and wants the best for all of humanity. This life force called God is an energy provided for the world to access at any time. The more we frequent this God-energy, the more alive, more discerning, self-actualized, and resplendent we become. We can more clearly identify, cultivate and utilize the gifts and abilities we have for the benefit of ourselves, others and the planet.

Before beginning a personal journey with the Christian mystics, it is helpful to understand, at least in generalities, what mysticism is, what Christian mysticism is, and how a Christian mystic is defined. Definitions vary with regard to mysticism. One simple, usable definition of mysticism is the, "immediate consciousness of the transcendent or ultimate reality or God." (mysticism.Dictionary.com)

According to Bernard McGinn, Christian mysticism is a form of spirituality that "concerns the preparation for, the consciousness of, and the reaction to the immediate or direct presence of God." (p2.) Therefore, Christian mysticism calls for actual work on the part of the mystic or seeker to get ready to be in the presence of God (preparation for), have an awareness of God in one's midst (consciousness of), and requires a subsequent response from the seeker that results from this preparation and awareness (reaction to). The tradition of Christian mysticism is as old as Christianity itself. The major emphasis associated with Christian mysticism is, "a transformation of the egoic self, the following of a path designed to produce more fully realized human persons created in the image and likeness of God and as such, living in harmonious communion with God, the Church, the rest of humanity and all creation, including oneself."[1] Harvey Egan states, "Christian mysticism is a way of life that involves the perfect fulfillment of loving God, neighbor, all God's creation, and oneself. It is the fundamental human process through which one becomes fully authentic by responding throughout life to a god who gives himself unconditionally as love and as the ultimate destiny of every person" (p.xviii). Authentic Christian mysticism has to do with a way of life that opens itself up to "otherness," to the God Source, albeit that lifestyle may come in an array of forms.

Emilie Griffin defines a Christian mystic as one "who is very close to God and includes those quiet, unassuming disciples who are transformed by being close to God through prayer and worship and service to others, those who are humble recipients of a gift of grace." She continues reminding us that Christian mystics do not ask to be mystics. Rather they wait humbly before God, admitting "their flaws and sinfulness and their need of God's redeeming grace." (p2) Clearly, being a Christian mystic requires work and accountability to both self and others.

Egan and other scholars identify Christian mystics as experiencing a three-fold process: "purgation, illumination and unitive life with God." (p.xviii)

Shawn Madigan writes, "A Christian mystic is one whose experiential awareness of Jesus Christ enables life to be lived with an increasing depth of faith-vision and love-dynamism." (p.3)

There is not one, singular definition for either Christian mysticism or the Christian mystic. The following three points however, seem to be characteristic of them both:

1) Mysticism is an awareness, a consciousness of the transcendent called God (Higher Power, Ultimate Reality, etc).

2) Christian mysticism includes not only an awareness of God, but a preparation takes place to be in that awareness, and then one has a reaction to being in the immediate presence of God. It is a way of life, a transformation that results in living authentically, loving God, others and self.

3) The Christian mystic is a person who is not only aware of but has an intimate relationship and dialogue with the Divine. Consequently, the Christian mystic lives harmoniously and authentically with God, others, oneself and all of creation, ultimately believing that one comes from God, belongs to God and will return to God.

The Christian mystics represented in this book are Trinitarian, biblically-oriented and committed to Christ's teachings. Some mystics have a Creation-centered theology which focuses on humanity created as being good. Some have a Redemptive-centered theology which is concerned with the fall of humankind from God's grace, and subsequently, the completion of Christ's death and resurrection to redeem humanity from that fall.

There are a variety of "schools" of mysticism reflected in the writings of the Christian mystics: "image mysticism, apophatic mysticism, Trinitarian mysticism and love mysticism" (Dupre' and Wiseman, p.7). As St. Paul writes, "Now there are varieties of gifts, but the same Spirit; and there are varieties of services, but the same Lord; and there are varieties of activities, but it is the same God who activates all of them in everyone. To each is given the manifestation of the Spirit for the common good." (1 Cor. 12: 4-7) So it goes, there is a wide-range of means for one to converge with God. No matter what means is taken, all of the mystics written about here have powerful testimonies to impart to us.

A curiosity about the messages of Christian mystics is their resemblance to the messages of modern day therapists, ecologists, some new age thought, and even the science of quantum physics. Examples are: Hildegard of Bingen's writings on ecology, gemology and herbal cures; St. Francis of Assisi's environmental, earth-day essay entitled "The Canticle of Brother Sun;" St. Ignatius of Loyola's modern day understanding of the importance of feelings for getting in touch with ourselves, our desires, and what we hope to become; Aelred of Rievaulx's description of the necessity of support persons (i.e. friends), about which he writes in his work; to the 20th century's Teilhard de Chardin with his understanding of the cosmos and its reciprocal connection to humanity and to all of creation. As we read the Christian mystics' writings, we find themes that complement what new science is now teaching:

1) The heart is literally the keeper of our feelings: "Since emotional processes can work faster than the mind, it takes a power stronger than the mind to bend perception, override emotional circuitry, and provide us with intuitive feeling instead. It takes the power of the heart." (Doc Childre, Founder, Institute of HeartMath);[2]

2) Our thoughts make a difference in how we feel and act (Scott, Elizabeth);[3] and

3) Feelings act as our internal guideposts, and are also integral to the new age "law of attraction." [4]

This all faintly reminds me of the scripture quote which seems to succinctly sum up this new age yet ancient thought: "you reap whatever you sow." (Ga.6:7)

May *Awakening the Mystic in You,* provide encouragement and new considerations for your life's journey. May you find benefit in the messages of these mystics as you determine what it is you wish to reap, by choosing what it is you wish to sow.

HOW TO USE THIS BOOK

As a meditation:
- Choose a quote and its reflection
- Read once
- Read again, out loud, slowly
- Question yourself as night draws near, to determine how the quote and reflection were applicable to your life during the day.

As a weekly journal to explore, connect, and transform your spiritual life:
Each week begin with a new topic (each is written by a different mystic) to create your spiritual journal. By the end of a year you will be filled with exciting, new insights based on your personal journey with each of the mystics.

USING THE SPIRITUAL JOURNAL: MINING THE TREASURE
Day 1 – Begin the search: *Gathering information.*
Read the mystic's message. Ponder the message throughout the day.
Day 2, Morning – Leave no stone unturned: *A different perspective.*
Read the reflection. Ponder the reflection throughout the day.
Day 2, Evening – Find the marker: *Enter into the experience.*
Write a few key words from the mystic's message or the reflection that hold a significant meaning for you. Create a symbol or image that describes these words.
Day 3 – Start the dig: *Investigate and articulate from a global view.*
Are the mystic's words and/or the reflection manifested in the world? If so, how?
Day 4 – Dig deeper: *Investigate and articulate from a personal view.*
Are the mystic's words and/or the reflection manifested in any part of your personal life? If so, how?
Day 5 – Eureka, You've found the treasure! *Imagine, sense, feel, experiment.*
Imagine if you applied the mystic's wisdom to all aspects of your life what it might be like. Which of your senses would be engaged? How so? How would it look? What would it sound like? How would you feel? How might your relationship improve with others, the planet, the God Source, and even your own self-regard?
Day 6 – Unlock the treasure chest: *Integrate and synthesize.*
Based on the last six days journeying with your mystic companion, write your own reflection of your mystic companion's message.
Day 7 – Claim Your Treasure: *Share your gift.*
By now, your inner mystic has awakened and is stirring. It is time to recognize this and write your very own message of light.

CHRONOLOGY OF THE MYSTICS

1st through 3rd century:
Origen, Antony of Egypt, Gregory of Nyssa, Augustine

4th through 8th century:
Pseudo-Macarius, John Climacus, Maximus Confessor, Amma Sarah

9th through 12th century:
Symeon the New Theologian, William of St. Thierry, Bernard of Clairvaux, Hildegard of Bingen, Aelred of Rievaulx, Francis of Assisi, Guigo II, Clare of Assisi

13th through 15th century:
Mechtild of Magdeburg, Bonaventure, Ramon Lull, Gertrude the Great, Meister Eckhart, John Ruusbroec Hadewijch of Antwerp, Richard Rolle, Johannes Tauler, Walter Hilton, Julian of Norwich, Catherine of Siena, The Anonymous Author, Thomas a'Kempis, Francisco de Osuna, Ignatius of Loyola

16th through 18th century:
Teresa of Avila, John of the Cross, Frances de Sales, Jeanne de Chantal, Angelus Silesius

19th through 21st century:
Therese of Lisieux, Gabrielle Bossis, Gemma Galgani, Elizabeth of the Trinity, Pierre Teilhard de Chardin, Karl Rahner, M. Faustina Kowalska, Simone Weil, Henri le Saux, Mother Teresa, Thomas Merton, Anthony De Mello, Henry Nouwen, Joan Chittister, Matthew Fox

AFFECTION

Bernard of Clairvaux

On Loving God

"As a drop of water
seems to disappear completely
in a chalice of wine,
so in the holy
it is necessary
that every human affection
in some ineffable way
will melt and flow totally
into the will of God."[1]

Reflection

When human affection is genuinely and honestly given, it is elevated to love; and because God is love, genuine human affection becomes elevated to the Holy.

Bernard of Clairvaux
1090-1153 CE

Bernard was born into a noble family, but to his parents' dismay became a monk at the age of 22. He eventually gained a reputation for holiness and wisdom while being involved in the political and ecclesiastical issues of Europe. Bernard was an abbot, church statesman, counselor to popes and kings and one of the most influential persons in Europe in the first half of the 12th century. He was renowned for the centrality of love in his spiritual writings and was the founder of Christianity's love mysticism movement.

APPROACHABILITY

Walter Hilton

The Scale of Perfection

"It may be prayer,
meditation,
reading,
or working,
but so long as the activity is one which
deepens the love of Jesus
in your heart and will and withdraws
your thoughts and affections
from worldly trivialities,
it is good."[1]

✦

Reflection

Once we acknowledge Jesus' love for us is the most excellent love to which we can ascribe, it does not matter whether we approach him through prayer, meditation, or by action. What matters is that we approach him

Walter Hilton
1330-1395 CE

Little is known about the early life of this English mystic. Hilton was considered by some to be one of the 14th century mystical giants. He led an eremitical life for many years prior to becoming a canon in about 1375. Even though Hilton lived in a time of great turmoil such as the Great Western Schism, the Hundred Year's War, the Peasants Revolt of 1381 and the Lollard movement, his writings are most serene. His famous *Scale of Perfection* offered such practical advice it became a favorite of the non-ordained when it was first published in 1494.

APPROVAL

Amma Sarah

Oral tradition

"If I prayed God that all people should approve of my conduct,
I should find myself a penitent at the door of each one,
but I shall rather pray
that my heart be pure toward all."[1]

✦

Reflection

Remember the adage, "you can please all of the people some of the time, and some of the people all of the time, but you can't please all the people all the time?" To people-please, we have to figure out what this one or that one wants then behave in a manner that tries to meet their expectations. It can leave us frustrated, feeling out of control and second-guessing ourselves. Better to focus on our interior life, that is, the intent of our own hearts. If we focus our hearts on purity, goodness and truth, then our exterior behavior will quite naturally follow suit.

Amma Sarah (Sara)
5th century

Amma Sarah, is one of the few desert mothers whose sayings are recorded. She probably lived around the Scetes desert in Egypt. She may have been a member of one of the new communities of ascetics that emerged at this time in the Egyptian desert.

7

BEING

Henri Le Saux

Saccidananda

"Being is essentially a call to life;
in its inward stillness,
it is a surging energy."[1]

✦

Reflection

Have you ever heard of the power of presence? Sometimes when a friend is grieving, your company is wanted. Not to exchange words, but to simply "be there." Just you, sitting next to your friend, quietly listening, a comfortable presence. There is power in such stillness. It is an energy no one sees, but is deeply and appreciably felt.

Henri Le Saux
1910-1973 CE

Henri was born in France, the oldest of eight children. He was ordained a priest at the age of 25. He taught Church history and patristics for the next 13 years. Henri had a love for India and joined Abbe Jules Monchanin in founding an ashram in Southern India. There he met a Hindu sage named Sri Ramana Maharishi who impressed him enormously. Henri participated enthusiastically in Hindu-Christian ecumenism. He took on the name Abhishiktananda which means, "the joy of the anointed one."

BELOVED

Ramon Lull

The Book of the Lover and Beloved

"The bird sang
in the garden of the Beloved.
The Lover came and said to the bird,
"If we do not understand one another in speech,
we can make ourselves understood by love,
for in your song
I see my Beloved before my eyes."[1]

✦

Reflection

The Lover in this story is you or me. The Beloved is God. God created the garden, the bird, and her song out of love for the Lover. God's love is the song that transcends and transforms us. If we willingly partake we will find God's love in the most unexpected places.

Ramon Lull
1232-1316 CE

Lull was born in Majorca (Spain) where there were a variety of religious traditions and ethnic groups. He became a page in the regal court and wrote love songs for his mistresses. He later married. After receiving a vision of Christ crucified, Lull felt compelled to share God's love with as many as would listen. He had a tolerant spirit and attempted to work with both the Christian and Muslim world.

CO-CREATION

Gabrielle Bossis

He and I

"I transform your prayers into my prayers.
But if you don't pray. . .
Can I make a plant that you haven't sown bear blossoms?"[1]

✦

Reflection

We are meant to be co-creators with the Divine. Create means, "to make something." This implies there is work involved. The Divine is always present and available to us, waiting for an invitation to join us in our work. Co-creation becomes a three-fold process: first we must invite the Divine to participate, second the work intended must be for the good, and lastly we must put our best foot forward as we complete the action that carries out our good intent. Such co-creation is a spiritually enhanced experience.

Gabrielle Bossis
1874-1950 CE

Born in France, Gabrielle was the youngest of four children, from a wealthy middle-class family. To those around her she was very outgoing and sociable, but she was contemplative as well. Even as a child she enjoyed talking with Jesus. Eventually, she obtained a nursing degree and served the poor and ill. At the age of 62 she became a successful playwright and actress, always continuing her conversations with Christ. She kept journals during her lifetime which were later published for the public's gain.

COSMOS

Matthew Fox

Wrestling with the Prophets

"The stars,
the one trillion galaxies,
the sun and the moon,
the mountains and waters
and forests and fish,
all have
their sacred and revelatory story to share."[1]

✧

Reflection

God's imprint is found in every animate and inanimate object on the Earth and in the Cosmos. If we want to be present to God, we must be present to the planet. There is an abundance of delights, enough for unending appreciation by each one of us. When we become observers, we bring life to that which is observed. Then we are ready to receive the story the Cosmos has to share.

Matthew Fox
1940-

Matthew Fox was first ordained as a Catholic priest of the Dominican order. He is a creation-centered theologian, an educator, and was the founding director of the Institute in Culture and Creation Spirituality at Holy Names College in Oakland. In 1988 under pressure from the Vatican he was silenced by his order for a year for some writings that deviated from the Vatican's viewpoint. When he continued writing, he was expelled from his Dominican Order and later excommunicated. He is now an Episcopalian priest and has authored numerous books.

DEEDS

Clare of Assisi

Testament

"Love one another
with the charity of Christ,
and let the love
which you have in your hearts
be shown outwardly
by your deeds."[1]

✦

Reflection

We have heard it said, "Actions speak louder than words." What we do tells the world who we really are and how we love.

Clare of Assisi
1196-1253 CE

Clare was born of a noble family in Assisi, Italy, and later became the first woman to write a religious rule. As a young woman, she desired to be a follower of Francis of Assisi. Against her family's wishes, one night she snuck out of her family home, met Francis and his followers so she could join his faction. Not knowing where to keep a young woman, Francis arranged for her to be taken in by the nearby Benedictine nuns. Clare was soon joined there with her biological sister before they moved into the church of San Damiano which Francis had refurbished. Clare eventually became abbess and remained at San Damiano the rest of her life. Her religious order of women became known as the Poor Clares to reflect their vow of poverty. Her written rule was approved by the pope two days prior to her death.

DELIGHT

Gertrude the Great

Part II of the Revelations of St. Gertrude

"... 'I (God) will receive you,
and inebriate you with the torrent of my celestial delight.'
When you had said these words,
my soul melted within me."[1]

✦

Reflection

Do you remember the children's song, "Would you Like to Swing on a Star? Your glee as a child imagining yourself swinging on that star? Now picture yourself as an astronaut in deep space gazing at the earth. Beyond words. Have you ever viewed the world from a mountain top? Magnificent. Perhaps drunk in the wonder of the Grand Canyon? Indescribable. Words are inadequate to express the splendor we feel when we imagine, are present to, or remember such extraordinary moments. Such moments of bliss and delight connect us with the divine.

Gertrude the Great
1256-1302 CE

Around the age of five, Gertrude was taken to the monastery at Helfta (Germany) to spend her childhood and receive an education. Gertrude was a quick learner and as a young woman decided to become a nun. Throughout her life, she would have frequent visions of Christ. Gertrude was a herald for Christ by explaining the meaning of her visions to all who would listen.

ENLIGHTENMENT

John Ruusbroec

The Little Book of Clarification

"All who experience and perceive
God's love
become interior and enlightened."[1]

✦

Reflection

Here are the keys to enlightenment: Live life to its fullest, love relentlessly as God loves you; until your love becomes like rain and pours down upon all whom you encounter.

John Ruusbroec
1293-1381 CE

Ruusbroec has been known as one of the greatest contemplative and mystical writers in the Christian tradition. He was born in South Brabant near Brussels, Belgium. At the age of 11, he went to live with his uncle, a canon at a Brussels cathedral. He was ordained at the age of 24 and was in close contact with the Beguine movement. He eventually became a member of the Augustinians.

EXPECTATION

Pseudo-Macarius

Homily XV

"For there, in the heart,
is the mind,
and all the faculties of the soul,
and its expectation;
therefore grace penetrates also
to all the members of the body."[1]

✦

Reflection

New research is confirming what the ancient ones knew: the heart may be the font of emotions, especially love. "The quantum electrical field of the heart is where love, or Spirit, enters the human system." [2] Open your heart to love and expect to receive God's penetrable gift of grace.

Psuedo-Macarius
Late 4th to early 5th Century

Pseudo Macarius was born in Mesopotamia. He became a monk in a desert community. His *Fifty Homilies* later influenced a wide-range of spiritual groups, both Catholic and Protestant.

FEELINGS

Ignatius of Loyola

Letters from St. Ignatius of Loyola

"God gives
or permits
an interior consolation
which casts out all uneasiness
and draws one
to a complete love of our Lord. . .
This consolation
points out and opens up
the way we are to follow
and points out the way we are to avoid."[1]

✦

Reflection

Feelings are the guideposts for life's journey. Pay close attention to the path you travel. If the path leads to genuine feelings of joy, peace, love, and kindness, these guideposts confirm you are living in God's light. If the path leads to persistent feelings of anger, anxiety, or mean-spiritedness, these guideposts confirm you have stepped onto a perilous path. With your very next step, follow the light. Step back onto the path of wholeness.

Ignatius of Loyola
1491-1556 CE

Ignatius was born in northern Spain of a noble household. He had five sisters and twelve brothers. At the age of 14 he was sent to his uncle at the royal court where he was trained to be a Spanish gentleman and courtier. As a trained soldier he was in his glory; he enjoyed gambling and cavorting with women. Then all changed when he received a serious leg wound in battle in 1521. As he convalesced, he read books on the life of Christ and the saints. His readings affected him so immensely he put behind his old lifestyle and was ordained a Catholic priest. Some call him the Father of spiritual direction. He was a church reformer, advisor to popes, kings, heads of state, and the founder of the Society of Jesus, commonly known as the Jesuits. His book, *Spiritual Exercises*, helped to change the history of spirituality and is widely used to this day.

FRIENDSHIP

Aelred of Rievaulx

On Spiritual Friendship

"The spiritual kiss is made
by affection of the heart;
by a mingling of spirits,
in the Spirit of God,
and through his own participation
it emits a celestial savor."[1]

✦

Reflection

Friends are gifts from God; Ponder the ways you love your friend: spiritually, emotionally and physically. Allow that love to be permeated and blessed by God. True friendships are heavenly ordained.

Aelred of Rievaulx
1110-1167 CE

One of three sons of a noble family in Hexham, England, Aelred was very popular and successful in the English Court of King Daniel the First. Even though he was popular with others, Aelred was not pleased with himself. He eventually became a Cistercian monk and gained a reputation for holiness and wisdom. He later became the abbot of the monastery at Rievaulx.

GROWTH

Henri Nouwen

The Wounded Healer

"For one with a deep-rooted faith in the value and meaning of life,
every experience holds a new promise,
every encounter carries a new insight
and every event brings a new message."[1]

Reflection

How beautiful and life-giving it is to view all life as an intermingling with the Divine. To understand such a relationship is to grow exponentially. We become enlightened with every petite exchange.

Henri Nouwen
1932-1996 CE

Nouwen, an internationally renowned priest and author, and respected professor wrote over 40 books on the spiritual life. Born in Nijkerk, Holland, Nouwen felt called to the priesthood at a young age. He was ordained in 1957 as a diocesan priest and studied psychology at the Catholic University of Nijmegen and at the Menninger Clinic. He went on to teach at the University of Notre Dame, and the Divinity Schools of Yale and Harvard. Nouwen lived and worked with the Trappist monks in the Abbey of the Genesee, and in the early 1980s he lived with the poor in Peru. In 1985 he was called to join L'Arche in Trosly, France, the first of over 100 communities founded by Jean Vanier where people with developmental disabilities live with assistance.

HEARTFELT

Richard Rolle

The Form of Living

"There is no need for you to be very eager
for a lot of books:
Hold on to love in heart and deed,
and you've got everything
which we can talk or write about."[1]

✦

Reflection

When you have love that comes from deep within, it is so palpable you can feel your heart pulsating. You are so gripped in love, you must act upon it, generously giving of yourself to the world around you. This love comes from no other than that Holy Mystery we call God. To recognize, accept and receive such love is the summit of one's life. Then you become the book of love.

Richard Rolle
1300-1349 CE

Richard was born in England and studied at Oxford. He became fascinated with theology and scripture studies. He left Oxford to lead an eremitical life. He became a prolific writer and in some circles is known as the Father of English literature. Richard was one of the most widely acclaimed spiritual writers up until the time of the Reformation.

HUMAN NATURE

Mechtild of Magdeburg

The Flowing Light of the Godhead

"This has God given to all creatures
to foster and seek
their own nature.
How then can I withstand mine?"[1]

✦

Reflection

If birds chirp and fly, fish swim effortlessly, and flowers are fragrant and beautiful, then what is it we humans are called to do and be? We are complex, multitalented beings who have the faculties of thought and the ability to love. We are called not to mediocrity, but rather to think great thoughts and love abundantly.

Mechtild of Magdeburg
1210-1297 CE

Mechtild was born of a noble family in Saxony. At the age of 12 she incurred a powerful experience with the Holy Spirit and from that moment on, she saw God in everything and everything in God. At the age of 23 she became a Beguine in Magdesburg. Years later she became affiliated with the Dominican order. She had extraordinary mystical experiences and was also outspoken against the corruption of clergy and those in the religious life. She was criticized and denounced as a heretic, but through it all, she held the church in high esteem. She fled to Helfta (Germany) which was an area widely known for its mystically talented writers, where she spent the rest of her life.

.

HUMILITY

Francisco de Osuna

Third Spiritual Alphabet

"Humility is the basis
for every devotion
and the root of every tree
that is to bear fruit."[1]

✛

Reflection

Humility is taken from the word, humus, that is, ground or earthy. Being humble is to recognize that we are grounded in God, divine life breathed into us. We come from God, and are journeying back to God. In humility we walk each step of our life's pathway with intention and awe.

Francisco de Osuna
1492-1540 CE

De Osuna was born in Seville, Spain at the time the last Moorish fortress fell, Columbus discovered the New World and many new ideas were developing. De Osuna authored over 500 works. He was considered a master of the spiritual life during the 16th century. His *Third Spiritual Alphabet* became an important guidebook for the future St. Teresa of Avila.

ILLUMINATION

Hadewijch of Antwerp

To Have Nothing But God

"The souls engulfed in God
who are thus lost in him
are illuminated on the side
by the light of Love,
as the moon receives its light
from the sun."[1]

✦

Reflection

When we consciously seek out God we become aware of his constancy, and illuminating love. Let us step out of the darkness of negativity into the light of the Divine.

Hadewijch of Antwerp
13th Century CE

In Belgium, Hadewijch lived as a Beguine (a religious community of women, but no vows were taken). The Beguines studied their faith, prayed together, gave spiritual direction, educated the community and cared for the sick and needy. Hadewijch was an exemplar of love mysticism. The theme or common thread of her writings is the soul's longing for the joy it receives through its experience of God's love. Her many writings indicate her intelligence, her lyrical and poetic genius, her literary range, deep spirituality and mysticism.

IMAGINATION

Symeon the New Theologian

Hymns of Divine Love

"As I was meditating. . .
suddenly, You appeared from above
and You shone brilliantly from the heavens
down into my heart."[1]

✦

Reflection

Imagine God as a light shining from beyond this realm, connecting deeply within you. Use this image to surround yourself in God's white light, whenever you feel afraid. Know you are protected by and held in God's love.

Symeon the New Theologian
942-1022 CE

Symeon was born in Galatia in Asia Minor, of a Byzantine[2] noble family and was educated at the imperial court in Constantinople. He entered a monastery at the age of 27 and later became an ordained priest. Even though he was rooted in the Eastern Christian tradition, the establishment thought him to be controversial, due to his zeal in stating theology was a mystical wisdom given by the Holy Spirit only after one went through purification through strict asceticism. Many of those in the Church hierarchy not living a life of asceticism were displeased by his arguments. He was vanquished for his views but was eventually exonerated by the Emperor and Patriarch.

INFUSION

Elizabeth of the Trinity

The Fulfillment of Christ's Prayer

"God is bending over us
with all his love,
day and night
longing to communicate with us,
to infuse his divine life into us
so as to make us into deified beings
who radiate him everywhere."[1]

✦

Reflection

The God-Source endlessly desires to infuse us with the sacred gifts of love, life and light. If we choose to accept these sacred gifts, love will spill over to all who are near; life will feel more precious; and we will become a light for the world. This is how we begin to bring a bit of Heaven to earth.

Elizabeth of the Trinity
1880-1906 CE

Born of a military family in Cher, France, Elizabeth's father died when she was seven years old. Still, she was outgoing and had a love for nature. She was a talented child and won first prize for her piano playing at the Conservatory in Dijon. At the age of 14 she began to think seriously about becoming a nun and at the age of 21 she entered the Carmelite community. She emphasized that God is all love, and to live in love and union with God it is necessary for one to remain steadily at the Source.

INSPIRATION

Francis de Sales

Finding God's Will for You

"Inspiration is a heavenly ray
that brings into our hearts
a warm light
that makes us the good,
and fires us on
to its pursuit."[1]

✦

Reflection

Formation of an idea may be heaven-sent if our intention is set upon God. Then our desire to bring the idea to fruition intensifies. It occupies our thoughts day and night. We are not satisfied until we exhaust all efforts to give the idea shape and form; as we become co-creators with the Divine.

Francis de Sales
1567-1622 CE

Francis believed in and was a proponent of Christian humanism. He was born of an aristocratic family in Savoy, France. He became Bishop of Geneva at the time when Catholics were actually banned from the city, during the Calvinist reformation. His way of teaching was to be an example of virtue, kindness and good behavior. He wrote for a wider audience of lay men and women and his book, the *Introduction to the Devout Life*, was then and is still a favorite among Christian readers. He co-founded (with Jeanne de Chantal) a women's religious order, the Visitation of the Blessed Mary, also known as the Visitation sisters.

INTIMACY

John of the Cross

The Living Flame of Love

"How gently and lovingly
You wake in my heart,
Where in secret You dwell alone;
And in your sweet breathing,
Filled with good and glory
How tenderly You swell my heart with love."[1]

✦

Reflection

Intimate union with God is an inexplicable experience; a mystical moment whereby we are completely awakened to the indwelling of God. Nothing rivals its exquisiteness. We are graced with pure goodness and left with pure desire.

John of the Cross
1542-1591 CE

Born in Spain, John's father was disowned by his wealthy family when he married a poor woman not of his social class. His father died when John was two years old. John lived an impoverished life. He entered a Carmelite monastery at the age of 20 and John eventually became fast friends with another mystic, Teresa of Avila. Together they co-founded the Discalced (shoeless) Carmelites, a reform movement in monasteries. He was so reviled by disgruntled members of his own religious community they imprisoned him for nine months. He was eventually released and subsequently held offices within his community.

INTUITION

The Anonymous Author

Cloud of Unknowing

"You may confidently rely
on God's gentle stirring of love in your heart
and follow wherever it leads you,
for it is your sure guide in this life
and will bring you to the glory of the next."[1]

✦

Reflection

If your intuition compels you to do some act of kindness, be assured you are being compelled by the Divine.

The Anonymous Author
1345-1386 CE

Many scholars consider this author, theologian and spiritual director to be a mystical genius of 14th century England. Yet the author's identity has never been established. He wrote and translated many books, the pinnacle being, "The Cloud of Unknowing." He taught a highly introspective form of mysticism.

INVITATION

Thomas Merton

The Inner Experience:
Kinds of Contemplation

"Walking down a street,
sweeping a floor,
washing dishes,
hoeing beans,
reading a book,
taking a stroll in the woods—
all can be enriched with contemplation
and with the obscure sense
of the presence of God."[1]

✦

Reflection

Invite God to be with you everyday even when you are performing a seemingly simple task. The mundane becomes sanctified when God shares the task with you.

Thomas Merton
1915-1968 CE

Born in France, Merton's father was a New Zealander, his mother an American and they both were artists. At the age of six, Merton's mother died and at the age of ten his father died. Merton received his education in France, England and Columbia University in the U.S. He lived an uninhibited life but at the same time he was intensely searching for meaning in his life. At the age of 23, he converted to Catholicism and three years later entered a Trappist monastery where his superior insisted he put pen to paper. His writings soon became internationally acclaimed.

LIFE

Gemma Galgani

The Life of the Servant of God

"Imagine
that you see a light of immense splendor,
that penetrates everything,
and at the same time
gives life and animation to all,
so that whatever exists
has its being from this light
and in it lives."[1]

✛

Reflection

How good it is to be born of the breath of God and bathed in the Holy light. When I arise from my sleep, let me look toward the light and give thanks for all life and for this moment. Let me praise the Source of all for my awakening.

Gemma Galgani
1879-1903 CE

Gemma was born in Italy; the fourth of eight children, her parents were very well-to-do. Gemma lived a short life suffering from ill health. Her mother died when she was only eight and her father died ten years later. The family went bankrupt and Gemma suffered extreme poverty. Her spiritual and mystical gifts became evident throughout her childhood beginning at age five. Not only experiencing visions and locutions, Gemma also received the stigmata. She became a Passionist nun six months prior to her death.

LISTEN

Angelus Silesius

The Cherubinic Wanderer

"The voice of God is heard.
Listen within and seek;
Were you but always silent,
He'd never cease to speak."[1]

✦

Reflection

As the drone of the audience in a theatre quiets itself when the curtain rises, one can hear a pin drop. So also, this is how we must quiet ourselves to listen for the voice of God.

Angelus Silesius
1624-1677 CE

Angelus was born in Poland to a well-to-do Lutheran family. He migrated to Germany and studied philosophy and medicine at various universities. He was appointed as the Court physician in Wurttenburg. Angelius converted to Catholicism and left his position as court physician. He eventually entered the Franciscan Order and was ordained a priest at the age of 37

LOVE

Thomas A' Kempis

My Imitation of Christ

"Nothing is sweeter than love;
nothing stronger,
nothing higher,
nothing more generous,
nothing more pleasant,
nothing fuller or better
in heaven or on earth;
for love proceeds from God
and cannot rest but in God
above all created things."[1]

✦

Reflection

Set your heart upon God for no one loves you any more. Learn to love as God loves; and strive to love no one any less.

Thomas A' Kempis
1380-1471 CE

Thomas was born in Germany. He entered a monastery where his older brother was Prior. Thomas represented the spiritual movement called the "new devotion," which stressed reading Scripture as a devotional and focused on love for Christ's humanity and passion. He wrote the great Catholic classic, "The Imitation of Christ. Thomas spent the rest of his life in the monastery transcribing and authoring many other works.

MERCY

M. Faustina Kowalska

Divine Mercy in My Soul

"God speaks: 'My daughter, know that My Heart is mercy itself.
From this sea of mercy, graces flow out upon the whole world.
No soul that has approached Me has ever gone unconsoled.
All misery gets buried in the depths of My Mercy,
and every saving and sanctifying grace flows from this fountain.
My daughter I desire that your heart be an abiding place of my mercy.
I desire that this mercy flow out upon the whole world
through your heart."[1]

✦

56

Reflection

When we allow Divine mercy to penetrate our hearts, we receive a Divine healing. Divine grace rushes into our hearts to mend our wounds; This grace is so abundant it spills over. The irony is as we impart this graceful abundance to others, we keep the Divine grace within. We then become empaths, full of mercy, compassion and grace which flow from our hearts to others.

M. Faustina Kowalska
1905-1938 CE

Faustina was born in a village in Poland. She was a pious child and began doing household work at the age of 14 without ever completing her elementary school education. At the age of 20 she entered the Congregation of the Sisters of Our Lady of Mercy. She was a sickly young woman and died from tuberculosis. She had kept a diary in which she recorded her conversations with Christ about his divine mercy which became a widely accepted Catholic devotion, entitled the Chaplet of the Divine Mercy

.

MIRACLES

Hildegard of Bingen

Scivias

"God brought forth from the universe
the different kinds of creatures,
shining in their miraculous awakening,
until each Creature was radiant
with the loveliness of perfection."[1]

✦

Reflection

If we make time to examine: a blade of grass or the petals of a rose, or if we envision our world as a miraculous creation, we begin to understand we have a connection to all of life. We begin to see the beauty and wonder of another person. We begin to recognize God's hand in all of creation.

Hildegard of Bingen
1098-1179 CE

Hildegard was an author, musical composer, abbess, founder of a monastery, religious reformer, scientist, herbalist, seer and mystic. She was born of a noble family and began having mystical visions at the age of five. Hildegard eventually joined the Benedictine community and became abbess. She wrote letters to popes, bishops, kings, emperors and people from all walks of life. She composed a multitude of liturgical songs, wrote books on pharmacology, medicine, natural history, homilies, a morality play, and many other writings describing her visions.

MOTHER EARTH

Francis of Assisi

The Canticle of Brother Sun

"Be praised, my Lord,
for our Sister Mother Earth,
who sustains and governs us,
and produces fruits
with colorful flowers and leaves."[1]

✧

Reflection

Mother Earth is a miraculous gift from which my needs are met and my senses stirred. How can I reciprocate?

Francis of Assisi
1182-1226 CE

Francis was born in Italy, into a wealthy middle-class family. He received a regular education but also learned Latin and French. Known as a fun-loving playboy he decided to become a soldier but later was captured and suffered as a prisoner of war for a short time. While on his way to Rome to fight for the pope, he had a revelation which stopped him in his tracks. This vision caused him to return to Assisi where he decided on a life of poverty and worked for the poor, much to his father's chagrin. Francis founded the Franciscan order and with Clare of Assisi, co-founded the order of sisters known as the Poor Clares. He is also one of the few who acquired the stigmata. People from all over were touched by his wisdom and holiness.

OPENNESS

Joan Chittister

Wisdom Distilled from the Daily

"To find God,
we must always be ready
to bend our heart
and change our paths
and open our minds."[1]

✦

Reflection

God reveals God-Self to us in innumerable and endless ways, often when we least expect it. We must ready ourselves to be open to all the possibilities God affords us. Being open to God creates an unobstructed energy flow from the head to the heart, which is beneficial to us and others.

Joan Chittister
1936-

Joan's father died when she was 3. She joined the Benedictine Sisters in Erie, Pennsylvania as a young woman and later was stricken with polio. It was four years before she walked again unaided. Joan is a social psychologist and communications theorist with a doctorate from Penn State University. She is a best-selling author and well-known international lecturer.

PHILOSOPHY

St. Anthony of Egypt

Oral Tradition

"A certain Philosopher asked St. Anthony:
'Father, how can you be so happy without the consolation of books?
Anthony replied,
My book, O Philosopher, is the nature of created things,
and anytime I want to read the words of God,
the book is before me."[1]

✦

Reflection

If we keep our minds open to the unexpected, sometimes we find answers to the great questions of life right in front of us. The universe is teeming with sacred and profound stories to share; stories about life, death, relationships and the ultimate mystery we call God. The universe with its analogies and metaphors, is ripe for the plucking, waiting for us to contemplate it for our own edification.

Anthony (Antony) of Egypt
251-356 CE

Saint Anthony the Great, also known as Anthony the Abbot, Anthony of Egypt, Anthony of the Desert, Anthony the Anchorite, Abba Antonius, and Father of All Monks, was an Egyptian Christian. He was a prominent leader among the Desert Fathers. Anthony lived in Alexandria for much of his life and spent many years in the desert as a monk.

PRESENCE

Guigo II

Twelve Meditations

"Let all my world
be silent in your presence, Lord,
so that I may hear what the Lord God
may say in my heart."[1]

✦

Reflection

In our busy, noisy world, to sit in silence may feel a bit foreign. Yet when we quiet our minds, slow ourselves down, focus on our breath, we feel more serene and tranquil. It is in this stillness, we are able to feel God's presence; and we are able to be present to God.

Guigo II
D.1188 CE

Guigo was a monk in the Carthusian Order. He eventually became the superior general of that order. Guigo like many western monastic mystics before him, depicted the soul as a chaste virgin who would know no husband except for Christ.

QUESTIONING

Simone Weil

Waiting for God
A Letter to Father J. M. Perrin, May 15, 1942

"For it seemed to me certain,
and I still think so today,
that one can never wrestle enough with God
if one does so out of pure regard for the truth."[1]

✦

Reflection

We learn about life from teachers, ministers, parents, friends, the media and a host of others. Somewhere along the way we learn to think for ourselves, to choose what we believe. As we progress in life, some things no longer make sense to us; to question, to search for the truth is a healthy exercise. To wonder, to lament, and to cajole with the Holy Mystery is part of our Holy evolution, until a day comes when we no longer have a need to ask such questions.

Simone Weil
1909-1943 CE

Weil was born in Paris in 1909 in an agnostic household from Jewish ancestry. She grew up in comfortable circumstances, as her father was a doctor. Her only sibling was the famous mathematician André Weil. She suffered throughout her life from severe headaches, sinusitis, and poor physical coordination but her condition did not limit her teaching and participation in the political movements of her time. She wrote extensively about the political movements of which she was a part and later about spiritual mysticism.

RELATIONSHIP

Teresa of Avila

The Book of Her Life

"Mental prayer. . .
is nothing else than an intimate sharing
between friends;
it means taking time frequently
to be alone with Him
who we know loves us."[1]

✦

Reflection

To develop intimate relationships, we share our innermost feelings, joys and sorrows with another. So it is with God who desires to be close to us. Much as we nurture our relationships with an old friend, so we must nurture our relationship with God. The result of this intimate sharing will be nothing short of a profound, restorative connection with the Source of all life.

Teresa of Avila
1515-1582 CE

Teresa was born in Spain, one of ten children. When she was 14 her mother died. She became difficult to manage and her father sent her to a Catholic boarding school. There she became so inspired she entered the Carmelite monastery when she was 20 years old. While at the monastery, Teresa had many health issues and also struggled with her prayer life. At the age of 40 she decided to surrender her struggles to God. She is known as a reformer of the Carmelite order and co-founder of the Discalced Carmelites. In 1970, she became the first woman to be proclaimed, "Doctor of the Church" by Pope Paul VI. Teresa authored many works, her masterpiece being, "The Interior Castle."

SEARCH

Augustine

Selected Writings

"Late have I loved you,
O Beauty,
so ancient and so new,
late have I loved you."[1]

✦

Reflection

O God, before the existence of time, you were. You loved me into existence and you love me even now. I have expended many years searching for you, only to find you have been with me all the while. Now I begin to grasp the enormity of your love for me, your overwhelming care for me. I need search no more.

Augustine
354-430 CE

Augustine was born in a small town in Algeria of a non-Christian father and Christian mother. He was well-educated and had a career as a rhetorician. He led a permissive lifestyle until he met Ambrose the bishop of Milan who became his teacher. Augustine was baptized into the Christian faith at the age of 33. He was ordained and later became Bishop of Hippo. Augustine was a pivotal person in the history of Christianity.

SENSIBILITY

Pierre Teilhard De Chardin

The Mystical Milieu

"If we are to build up in ourselves,
for God,
the structure of sublime love,
we must first of all
sharpen our sensibility."[1]

✦

Reflection

How do we sharpen our sensibility? We can become like a child who plays hide and seek with God. We can discover God everywhere, in all things; where we go, in what we see, smell, hear, touch and taste. See how elated we feel when we come to our "senses" and find the purpose of our search?

Pierre Teilhard De Chardin
1881-1955 CE

Pierre was born in France, his father a farmer. Pierre was ordained a priest at the age of 30. As a Jesuit he was well-trained in the classics, theology and philosophy. He was especially fond of natural sciences, especially geology and paleontology. Receiving his doctorate in paleontology, he conducted numerous scientific experiments, archeological expeditions, took part in the discovery of Peking man, and was a prolific writer.

SENSUALITY

Origen

The Mystical Senses

"For just as in the body
there are different senses of tasting and seeing,
so are there. . . . different faculties of perception.
One of them is the seeing
and contemplating power of the soul,
the other, a faculty of taste
for receiving spiritual food."[1]

✦

Reflection

Senses play a role in spirituality. The soul "sees" things and interprets them as bringing peace or upheaval to the sentient being. The soul hears the sounds of nature and smells its bouquet. This consciousness allows the soul to interpret such wonders as Divine gifts. Senses enhance our soulful experiences.

Origen
185-254 CE

Origen was the oldest of seven children born in Alexandria, Egypt. His father was martyred for the Christian faith when Origen was a teenager. Origen began a school for grammar to support his family. He had a reputation for learning and holiness. Several of his views were condemned by the Church in the year 553. However, his Christian genius was recognized during the Renaissance and revived in the 20th century.

SERENITY

Maximus Confessor

The Four Hundred Chapters on Love
Fourteenth Century

"The unutterable peace of the holy angels
is attained by these two dispositions:
love for God and love for one another.
This holds true as well for all the saints
from the beginning."[1]

✦

Reflection

Genuine peace is sacred; it comes from Eternal Love. It is our choice to allow this loving energy to envelop and penetrate our being. To choose to be in sacred peace, we must permit ourselves to become aware of the Holy Presence and allow it to act upon us. This allows us to remove any obstacles we previously created which impeded the transmission of Divine loving energies to us and to others through us. Once we choose to and do remove the obstructions, we can enter into a sacred serenity.

Maximus Confessor
580-662 CE

As an aristocrat in Constantinople, Maximus received a broad Christian and humanistic education. He was in the service of Emperor Heraclius. After three years in such service, Maximus made a radical change and joined the monastery at Chrysopolis. In 626, due to the Persian invasion, he was forced into exile moving from Crete to Cyprus to North Africa. He became one of the greatest theologians of the Byzantine Church.

SHARING

Catherine of Siena

The Dialogue

"If you had a burning lamp,
and all the world came to you for light,
the light of your lamp would not be diminished by the sharing.
Yet each person who shared it would have the whole light.
True, each one's light would be more or less intense
depending on what sort of material
each one brought to receive the fire."[1]

✦

Reflection

We are all recipients of the "burning lamp," a precious light that was gifted to us before we were born; that illuminates our hearts and minds, and leads to goodness and love. We have an unspoken commission to keep the lamp stoked. When the lamp is stoked it burns brightly and attracts others to its light. May we share our light unselfishly with others. May we keep our flame burning brightly.

Catherine of Siena
1347-1380 CE

Catherine was born in Italy of a prosperous family, the 24th of 25 children. She had visions of Christ beginning at the age of six. At the age of 15, to avoid the marriage expected of her by her parents, she cut off her hair to make herself undesirable to her suitors. She soon became a member of the Dominican order where she attended to the sick and the poor while she lived at home. She became quite renowned for her dedication to others and soon had a following of people. Even though Catherine had no formal education, she became one of the greatest teachers in the Catholic Church, so well-regarded, the pope accepted her assistance to return to Rome from Avignon which helped end the travesty of the papacy at the time.

SIGNIFICANCE

Johannes Tauler

Sermon 47

"Every service or activity,
however insignificant,
is a grace,
and it is the same spirit
which produces them all
for the use and profit of mankind."[1]

✦

Reflection

"The fluttering of a butterfly's wings can effect climate changes on the other side of the planet" according to scientist, Paul Ehrlich. Therefore, any little thing we do, every seemingly small service or action we accomplish for others, will have a great, far-reaching significance; one which we cannot imagine and may never see. But know this: Every service and action for others has God's blessing and signature. It is that important.

Johannes Tauler
1300-1361 CE

Johannes was born into a well-to-do family in Strasbourg. He joined the Dominican order at the age of 15. Johannes became one of the most influential preachers and spiritual directors in the Rhineland during the 14th century.

SILENCE

Mother Teresa

A Simple Path

"I always begin my prayer
in silence,
for it is in the silence of the heart
that God speaks."[1]

✦

Reflection

Have you ever sat quietly beside a creek listening to the water bubbling over the stones, the sparrows playfully singing out, the leaves fluttering in the breeze? Nature sounds yet our soul is silenced. Our ears attend to the present moment, alert. Now we are ready to hear God.

Mother Teresa
1910-1997 CE

Mother Teresa was born Agnes Bojaxhiu in Yugoslavia. She was one of three children. Her father worked as a grocer while her mother stayed home and cared for the children. As a teenager she was very involved in a Christian youth group and had the desire to become a missionary. Agnes learned English while at the Loretto Abbey in Dublin, Ireland in 1928. She made her final vows as a Loretto sister in 1937, in India, where she had been sent and took on the name of Teresa. She taught high school and later became the school principal. She received an inspiration from God to work for the poor, so she received permission to leave the cloister where she traded in her traditional habit for a white sari. Mother Teresa studied nursing, founded the Congregation of the Missionaries of Charity and lived with the poor in Calcutta, India.

SIMPLICITY

Jeanne de Chantal

Letter of Spiritual Direction to Her Brother Andre Fremyot,
Archbishop of Bourges

"As for prayer,
don't burden yourself with making considerations;
neither your mind nor mine is good at that.
Follow your own way of speaking to our Lord
sincerely, lovingly, confidently,
and simply, as your heart dictates."[1]

✦

Reflection

Feeling my prayer life to be unsatisfactory, I once told my friend, "I need help praying. I want to pray spontaneously, like you; not just say the formal prayers I learned as a child." She said, "Just pray from your heart. Think about what it is you want to pray about and just say it." I felt, "less than," comparing my lack of finesse in prayer with others who were so eloquent. The energy I expended worrying about the way I prayed was precious energy wasted away. I realize now that prayer is best done when it comes from the heart, no frills necessary.

Jeanne de Chantal
1572-1641 CE

Jeanne (Jane) was born in Dijon, France. Her mother died before Jeanne was two years old. Jeanne was raised by her father an attorney, and her aunt. Jeanne and her two siblings became well-educated in financial, legal and practical matters. She married a wealthy man and oversaw his estate. They had four children but soon she was widowed. She met Francis de Sales and the two became great friends. Together, they envisioned a community of mothers with their children, praying together, and visiting the sick and the poor. Their vision turned to reality when they established the Catholic community known as the Visitation sisters

.

SIN

Meister Eckhart

Counsels on Discernment

"If it should ever be
that your great sins drive you so far off
that you cannot think of yourself
as being close to God,
still think of him as being close to you."[1]

✦

Reflection

When we are in relationship with God, we invite the Holy Presence to abide in us. When we commit serious wrongdoings, we essentially drive that Presence out of our hearts. Make no mistake though, God patiently waits for us to desire and bid the Divine one's return. It is our choice. May we choose wisely.

Meister Eckhart
1260-1328 CE

Born in the Rhineland, Eckhart entered the Dominican order at the age of 15. He studied at Europe's prestigious universities and received his Master's degree from the University of Paris, hence the name, "Meister." He spent several years teaching theology and was renowned as a preacher and spiritual director. He held positions of high authority, but in 1326 the Franciscan Archbishop of Cologne charged him with heresy. Eckhart defended himself but died before his case was concluded. Some say the condemnation was in part due to the Franciscan-Dominican theological controversy at that time. He has been misunderstood by many but a resurgence in studying Eckhart's works has occurred in recent times.

STEADFAST

Therese of Lisieux

Story of a Soul

"The little bird,
with bold surrender,
wishes to remain gazing
upon its Divine Sun.
Nothing will frighten it,
neither wind
nor rain,
nor dark clouds."[1]

Reflection

Picture God's love for us as the Sun, its rays always fixed upon us. Even when clouds cover it, it is there shining brightly. Even when the earth turns and night falls, it is still there shining steadfastly. And in the morning, we can throw open the shutters and welcome the One who is there shining just for us.

Therese of Lisieux
1873-1897 CE

Born in France, Therese was the youngest of nine children, four of whom died before she was born. Both of her parents had unsuccessfully attempted to enter religious orders prior to their marriage. They participated in an active faith-filled life and engaged the entire family in service to the poor and sick. Therese was only 4 years old when her mother died. Therese became very sickly at the age of ten, but was miraculously cured while praying at the Our Lady of Victories statue. She entered a Carmelite monastery at the age of 15. Therese is renowned for her "little way," measuring sanctity not by great deeds, but through the quality of love in the duties of daily life.

SURRENDER

Karl Rahner

Encounters with Silence

"When I abandon myself in your love,
my God,
then You are my very life,
and your Incomprehensibility
is swallowed up
in love's unity."[1]

✦

Reflection

If I surrender completely to God's love, then the Mystery called God no longer needs to be solved. Instead, remarkably, I find myself as an inextricable element of that Divine Mystery, as a drop of water is to the sea.

Karl Rahner
1904-1984 CE

Karl was the middle child of seven children, born in West Germany. His father was a teaching professor. Karl became a Jesuit priest and one of the great mystical theologians of the 20th century. He taught theology, lectured and was a prolific writer. His influence on the Catholic church' Second Vatican Council (1962-1965) was hugely significant.

TRANSFORMATION

Bonaventure

The Soul's Journey Into God

"No one comes to wisdom
except through grace,
justice
and knowledge."[1]

✦

Reflection

We come to wisdom when we admit our transgressions, are willing to accept the consequences for what we have done or failed to do, have a firm desire to change our ways, and ask God to transform us. God is always ready to attend to us with mercy and loving kindness; to assist us in our transformation. All we need do is ask and follow the guidance we open ourselves to receive.

Bonaventure
1217-1274 CE

Bonaventure was born in Italy of a well-to-do family. He studied at the University of Paris and entered the Franciscan order at the age of 26. He later became a lecturer at the University of Paris and was the author of numerous scholastic papers. He was selected the General of the Franciscan order where he wrote many spiritual works. He became a cardinal in the Catholic Church and played a major role in Church reform.

TRUST

Julian of Norwich

Revelations of Divine Love

"God wishes us to love
and be pleased with him
and put great trust in him,
and all shall be well."[1]

✦

Reflection

It is mind-boggling, when bad things happen to innocent people and we naturally ask why? Often we worry, "will something bad happen to me or my family today?" God intimates there is no need for worry. Intellectually, we know worry is not a way to fix anything and lends to further anxiety, and health issues. Still, we revert to worrying. How do we not worry? We must let go of control, judgment, and manipulative tactics. We surrender all of this negativity to the Universal Source. When a worrisome thought comes to mind, release it. Replace it with a positive thought. Stay in the present moment. Everything is to be made whole in the Divine's own time and way, not necessarily ours, a mystery to be sure. Even in the darkest moments, trust in God, "all shall be well."

Julian of Norwich
1342-1423 CE

We know very little about Julian of Norwich, not even her real name. We do know that she was an anchorite who lived in a room attached to the Church of St. Julian in Norwich, England. On her deathbed, while pondering a crucifix, Julian had a series of visions of and conversations with Christ. She rapidly recovered from her illness and recorded what she saw. As she prayerfully reflected on these visions twenty years later, she wrote a "Long Text" providing further explanation and commentary on her revelations from God. Julian has the claim of being the first woman writer in the English language.

UNION

John Climacus

The Hesychast

"Prayer is by nature a dialogue
and a union of a *person* with God.
Its effect is to hold the world together.
It achieves reconciliation with God. . .
Make the effort to rise up, or rather,
to enclose your mind
within the words of your prayer;
and if, like a child,
it gets tired and falters,
raise it up again."[1]

✦

Reflection

Converging with the Divine we discover that we are not the end all, rather we are beautiful, unique and integral parts of the Whole. We are necessary to its form, evolution and restoration. The potentiality from this union is nothing less than transformational. Therefore it is a moral imperative to make time for this Divine union.

John Climacus
579-649 CE

Very little is known about the early life of John. It is known that he spent 40 years in solitude in the Sinai desert before he became the abbot of the monastery on Mount Sinai. He was of the hesychastic (ancient monastic Eastern Orthodox form) tradition. In his famous work, *The Ladder*, the 30 chapters of the book each depict Christ's 30 years on earth. Climacus is also known as John Scholasticus.

VITALITY

William of St. Thierry

The Golden Epistle

"When the object of thought is God
and the things which relate to God and the will
reaches the stage at which it becomes love,
the Holy Spirit,
the Spirit of life
at once infuses itself by way of love
and gives life to everything."[1]

✦

Reflection

God is love. Love is transformative. When we become one with God in love, our prayers and thoughts become spirit-filled. We taste with zest the goodness of God. Our love and desire for God is amplified. Everything around us seems to pulsate with vitality.

William of St. Thierry
1085-1148 CE

William was born into a noble family in Liege and received an excellent education. He entered the Benedictine abbey where he became friends with Bernard of Clairvaux. William became a Cistercian monk in his quest for deeper solitude and contemplation.

WISDOM

Anthony De Mello

One Minute Wisdom

"What makes one a genius?"
The Master answered,
"the ability to recognize
a butterfly in a caterpillar,
the eagle in an egg,
the saint in a selfish human being."[1]

✦

Reflection

When we begin to appreciate the caterpillar or the egg, we take our first steps toward wisdom. We concede that there is much more to know than our eyes can see.

Anthony De Mello
1931-1987 CE

Anthony was a priest and psychotherapist who became widely known for his books on spirituality. He traveled to many countries to study and teach and he eventually established a prayer center in India. In 1998, Cardinal Joseph Ratzinger, (now Pope Benedict XVI), then Prefect of the Congregation for the Doctrine of the Faith, wrote a Vatican Notification concerning De Mello's writings declaring his "positions are incompatible with the Catholic faith and can cause grave harm." (Vatican.va) Some editions of his books were supplemented with this insertion of caution: "The books of Father Anthony de Mello were written in a multi-religious context to help the followers of other religions, agnostics and atheists in their spiritual search, and they were not intended by the author as manuals of instruction of the Catholic faithful in Christian doctrine or dogma." (Thomas, T.K.)

WONDER

Gregory of Nyssa

Commentary on the Song of Songs

"As God continues to reveal Himself,
man continues to wonder;
and he never exhausts his desire to see more,
since what he is waiting for
is always more magnificent,
more divine,
than all that he has already seen."[1]

✦

Reflection

God is omnipotent, full of marvel. The deeper we fall in love with God, the more wondrous are God's manifestations. As we draw closer to God, we see the world with more clarity; it becomes more vibrant. Each day can be more astonishing than the last.

Gregory of Nyssa
335-385 CE

Gregory was born into a family of great saints. His father was St. Basil the Elder; his sister, St. Macrina; his brothers, St. Basil the Great and St. Peter of Sebate. Gregory was ordained as a lector but left before becoming a priest, choosing instead to get married working as a rhetorician. Sometime thereafter he had a change of heart, joined the priesthood and eventually became a bishop. Gregory was well-regarded for his knowledge, wisdom and his numerous writings.

ENDNOTES

Brief quotations have been taken from the following sources; the complete details are provided in the Bibliography

INTRODUCTION
1. http://en.wikipedia.org/wiki/Christian_mysticism#Notes_and_references
2. Childre, Doc. www.heartmath.org/research-science-of-the-heart/
   "Numerous experiments have now demonstrated that the messages the heart sends the brain affect our perceptions, mental processes, feeling states and performance in profound ways. Our research suggests that the heart communicates information relative to emotional state (as reflected by patterns in heart rate variability) to the cardiac center of the brain stem (medulla)..."
3. Scott, Elizabeth. http://stress.about.com/od/positiveattitude/ht/attraction.htm
4. www.todayisthatday.com/lawofattraction.html
   "The only way to attract what you desire in life is to allow yourself to understand what it would feel like to have what you want, to allow yourself to believe that you will have it, that you deserve it, and by focusing on those positive feelings and beliefs on a consistent basis."

AELRED OF RIEVAULX
1. Aelred of Rievaulx: On Spiritual Friendship. 2:10-11
   The quote is paraphrased from the original quote: "The spiritual kiss is ... made. ... by the affection of the heart... by a mingling of spirits... it emits a celestial savor"

AMMA SARAH
1. Beasley-Topliffe, Keith. *Seeking A Purer Christian Life.* p. 58

ANGELUS SILESIUS
1. Angelus Silesius. *Angelus Silesius: The Cherubinic Wanderer.* 5: 330, 124.

ANTHONY DE MELLO
1. DeMello, Anthony. *One Minute Wisdom.* p. 206
   This quote is paraphrased from the original quote: "... said the Master... and what makes one a genius... Recognize what? The butterfly in a caterpillar; the eagle in an egg; the saint in a selfish human being."

ANTHONY OF EGYPT
1. Merton, Thomas. *The Wisdom of the Desert.* p. 139

AUGUSTINE
1. St. Augustine. *Saint Augustine Confessions. Oxford World Classics.* p.201

BERNARD OF CLAIRVAUX

1. Bernard of Clairvaux. *On Loving God. Treatises.* 28
This quote is paraphrased from the original quote: "As a drop of water seems to disappear completely in a chalice of wine . . . so in the holy it is necessary that every human affection in some ineffable way will melt and flow totally into the will of God."

BONAVENTURE

1. Bonaventure. *Bonaventure:* The Soul's Journey into God, the Tree of Life. *The Life of St. Frances.* P. 63

CATHERINE OF SIENA

1. Noffke, Suzanne, Ed. *Catherine of Siena. The Dialogue, Classics of Western Spirituality.* P. 207

CLARE OF ASSISI

1. Petroff, Elizabeth, Ed. *Medieval Women's Visionary Literature.* p. 245

ELIZABETH OF THE TRINITY

1. Elizabeth of the Trinity. "French, letter 294." *Elizabeth of the Trinity, Complete Works,* Vol. II
This quote is paraphrased from the original quote: "God. . ."

FRANCES DE SALES

1. De Sales, Frances. *Finding God's Will for You..* p. 43

FRANCIS OF ASSISI

1. Francis of Assisi. *The Little Flowers of St. Francis.* pp. 317-318

FRANCISCO DE OSUNA

1. de Osuna, Francisco. *Francisco de Osuna—Third Spiritual Alphabet..* pp. 494-496, 512-513

GABRIELLE BOSSIS

1. Bossis, Gabrielle. *He and I.* p. 27

GEMMA GALGANI

1. Father Germanicus, C.P. *The Life of the Servant God Gemma Galgani: An Italian Maiden of Lucca.* p. 227

GERTRUDE THE GREAT

1. Gertrude the Great. *www.my.homewithgod.com/gertrude/book*

GREGORY OF NYSSA

1. "Commentary on the Song of Songs.Sermon 12." *Gregory of Nyssa: The Life of Moses.*

GUIGO II

1. Bynum, Caroline. *Jesus as Mother: Studies of the High Middle Ages.* p. 73

HADEWIJCH OF ANTWERP

1. Hadewijch of Antwerp. *Hadewijch, the Complete Works* . Trans. Mother Columba Hart, O.S. B. Mahwah, NJ: Paulist Press, 1980. pp. 88-89

HENRI LE SAUX

1. Le Saux, Henri. *Saccidananda: A Christian Approach to Advaitic Experience.* pp. 174-181

HENRI J.M. NOUWEN

1. Nouwen, Henri J.M. *The Wounded Healer.* p.75

HILDEGARD OF BINGEN

1. Hildegard of Bingen. *Creation and Christ. The Wisdom of Hildegard of Bingen.* p. 48
   This quote is paraphrased from the original quote: "He brought forth form the universe the different kinds of creatures, shining in their miraculous awakening. . until each creature was radiant with the loveliness of perfection. . . "

IGNATIUS OF LOYOLA

1. Ignatius of Loyola. "Letter to Sister Teresa Rejadell." *Letters of St. Ignatius Loyola.* p.21
   This quote is paraphrased from the original quote: "Lord . . . gives or permits. . . an interior consolation which casts out all uneasiness and draws one to a complete love of our Lord. . . .This consolation points out and opens up the way we are to follow and points out the way we are to avoid."

JEANNE DE CHANTAL

1. Francis de Sales and Jane de Chantal. "Francis de Sales, Jane de Chantal: letters of Spiritual Direction." *The Classics of Western Spirituality.* pp. 201-3

JOAN CHITTISTER

1. Chittister, Joan. *Wisdom Distilled from the Daily.* p. 141

JOHN OF THE CROSS

1. John of the Cross. *The Collected Works of St. John of the Cross.* pp. 578-579

JOHANNES TAULER
1. Tauler, Johannes. *Johannes Tauler: Sermons.* pp. 153-157

JOHN CLIMACUS
1. Climacus, John. *John Climacus: The Ladder of Divine Ascent..* p. 103

JOHN RUUESBROEC
1. Ruusbroec, John. *John Ruusbroec: The Spiritual Espousals and Other Works.* (Part Three: Union With out Difference, B. These Three Unions as the Fulfill ment of Christ's Prayer) p. 267
This quote is paraphrased from the original quote: "All who experience and perceive God's love become interior and enlightened

JULIAN OF NORWICH
1. Julian of Norwich. *Revelation of Divine Love.* p. 155
This quote is paraphrased from the original quote: "He wishes us to love and be pleased with him and put great trust in him, and all shall be well."

KARL RAHNER
1. Rahner, Karl. "God of my Life." *The Practice of Faith: A Handbook of Contemporary Spirituality.* pp 3-10
This quote is paraphrased from the original quote: "When I abandon myself in your love, my God, then You are my very life, and your Incomprehensibility is swallowed up in love's unity."

M. FAUSTINA KOWALSKA
1. Kowalska, M. Faustina. *Divine Mercy in my Soul: The Diary of the Servant of God Sister M. Faustina Kowalska, Perpetually Professed Member of the Congregation of Sisters of our Lady of Mercy,* Entry #1777

MATTHEW FOX
1. Fox, Matthew. *Wrestling with the Prophet..* p. 218

MAXIMUS CONFESSOR
1. Maximus Confessor. *Maximus Confessor, Selected Writings.* pp. 1-13

MECHTILD of MAGDEBERG
1. Mechtild of Magdeberg. *The Revelations of Mechtild of Magdeburg: The Flowing Light of God.* pp. 205

MEISTER ECKHART
1. Meister Eckhart. *Everything As Divine: The Wisdom of Meister Eckhart, p.62*

MOTHER TERESA
1. Mother Teresa. *Mother Teresa. Meditations from a Simple Path.* p. 5

ORIGEN
1. Urs von Balthasar, Hans. *Origen-Spirit and Fire: A Thematic Study of His Writings.* pp 220-221

PIERRE TEILHARD DE CHARDIN
1. Soltes, Ori. *Mysticism in Judaism, Christianity, and Islam: Searching for Oneness.*p.265
   This quote is paraphrased from the original quote: "If. . . to build up in . . . for God, the structure of sublime love, . . . must first of all sharpen his sensibility."

PSEUDO-MACARIUS Homily XV
1. Pseudo-MaCarius.*Fifty Spiritual Homilies of St. Macarius the Great.* pp.1-2, 10-112. <www.selfgrowth.com/articles/heart-centeredness.html>*"The quantum electrical field of the heart is where love, or Spirit, enters the human system."*

RAMON LULL
1. Lull, Ramon. *The Book of the Lover and Beloved.* #27.

RICHARD ROLLE
1. Rolle, Richard. Richard Rolle:The English Writings.*Classics of Western Spirituality series.* p.173

SIMONE WEIL
1. "A Letter fo Father J.M. Perrin, May 15, 1942, by Simone Weil. God In His Mercy.*" Parabola.*Vol.33 Number 2, Summer 2008. p. 55

SYMEON THE NEW THEOLOGIAN
1. Symeon the New Theologian. *Hymns of Divine Love by Symeon the New Theologian..* pp. 135-138
2. "byzantine." *WordNet® 3.0.* Princeton University. 15 Dec. 2008. <Dictionary.com http://dictionary.reference.com/browse/byzantine>.

TERESA OF AVILA
1. Teresa of Avila. "The Book of Her Life.*" The Collected Works of St. Teresa of Avila- I.* Trans. p. 67

THE ANONYMOUS AUTHOR, CLOUD OF UNKNOWING
1. Author of the Cloud of Unknowing. *The Assessment of Inward Stirrings, in The Pursuit of Wisdom and Other Works*, p. 100
   This quote is paraphrased from the original quote: "You may confidently rely on. . . .gentle stirring of love in your heart and follow wherever it leads you, for it is your sure guide in this life and will bring you to the glory of the next."

THERESE OF LISIEUX
1. Therese of Lisieux. *Story of a Soul: The Autobiography of St. Therese of Lisieux.* pp. 192-200 , 276-277
   This quote is paraphrased from the original quote: "This little bird. . . with bold surrender, . . . wishes to remain gazing upon its Divine Sun. Nothing will frighten it, neither wind nor rain, . . . dark clouds"

THOMAS A' KEMPIS
1. Thomas A' Kempis. *My Imitation of Christ.* pp. 172-174.

THOMAS MERTON
1. Merton, Thomas. "The Inner Experience: Kinds of Contemplation IV," *Cistercian Studies.* VIII, 4, 1983. pp. 294-297.

WALTER HILTON
1. Hilton, Walter. *The Scale of Perfection.* pp. 71-76

WILLIAM OF ST. THIERRY
1. William of St. Thierry. *The Golden Epistle.* p. 92

BIBLIOGRAPHY

Aelred of Rievaulx. *Aelred of Rievaulx: On Spiritual Friendship*. Trans. Mary Eugenia Laker, S.S.N.D. Washington DC: Cistercian Publications, 1974.

Augustine.*Saint Augustine Confession, Oxford World Classics*. Trans. Henry Chadwick.. Oxford: Oxford University Press, 1991

Author of the Cloud of Unknowing. *The Assessment of Inward Stirrings, in The Pursuit of Wisdom and Other Works* Trans. and Ed. James A. Walsh, S.J. Mahwah, NJ: Paulist Press, 1988.

Beasley-Topliffe, Keith. *Seeking A Purer Christian Life*. Upper Room Books. Nashville, 2000.

Bernard of Clairvaux. *On Loving God*. Treatises. 3 vols. Trans. Michael Casey et al. Kalamazoo, MI: Cistercian Publications, 1969.

Bonaventure. *Bonaventure: The Soul's Journey into God, The Tree of Life, The Life of St. Frances*. Trans. Ewert Cousins. Mahwah, NJ: Paulist Press, 1978.

Bossis, Gabrielle. *He and I*. ed. and trans. Evelyn M. Brown. Sherbrooke, Canada: Editions Paulines, 1969.

Brandon, Diane. "Heart-Centeredness."*The Online Self-Improvement Encyclopedia.* <www.selfgrowth.com/articles/heart-centeredness.html>*"The quantum electrical field of the heart is where love, or Spirit, enters the human system."*

Bynum, Caroline. *Jesus as Mother: Studies of the High Middle Ages*. Berkeley: University of California Press, 1982

byzantine. *WordNet® 3.0*. Princeton University. 15 Dec. 2008. <Dictionary.com http://dictionary.reference.com/browse/byzantine>.

Catherine of Siena. *Catherine of Siena. The Dialogue, The Classics of Western Spirituality*. Ed. Suzanne Noffke. NY: Paulist Press, 1980.

Chittister, Joan. *Wisdom Distilled from the Daily*. NY: Harper Collins, 1990.

Climacus, John. *John Climacus: The Ladder of Divine Ascent*. intro. Kallistos Ware. Trans. Colm Luibheid and Norman V. Russell. Mahwah, NJ: Paulist Press, 1982.

De Mello, Anthony. *One Minute Wisdom*. NY: Image Books. Doubleday, 1988.

de Osuna, Francisco. *Francisco de Osuna-Third Spiritual Alphabet*. Trans. Mary E. Giles Mahwah, NJ: Paulist Press, 1981.

De Sales, Frances. *Finding God's Will for You*. Manchester, NH: Sophia Institute Press, 1998.

Doc Childre. http://www.heartmath.org/research-science-of-the-heart/Dupre', Louis and James A. Wiseman, O.S.B. Editors. *Light from Light*. Second Edition. Mahwah, NJ: Paulist Press, 2001.

Egan, Harvey. *An Anthology of Christian Mysticism.*Second Edition. Collegeville, MN: The Liturgical Press, 1996.

Elizabeth of the Trinity. *French, letter 294. Elizabeth of the Trinity, Complete Works, Vol. II*, ed. Conrad de Meester, O.C.D. Trans. Sr. Elizabeth, O.C.D. Washington DC: Institute of Carmelite Studies, 1990.

Father Germanicus, C.P. *The Life of the Servant God Gemma Galgani: An Italian Maiden of Lucca*. Trans. A.M. O'Sullivan, O.S.B. St Louis. B. Herder, 1913.

Fox, Matthew. *Wrestling with the Prophets*. NY: Harper Collins, 1995.

Francis de Sales, Jane de Chantal. *Francis de Sales, Jane de Chantal: Letters of Spiritual Direction*. Trans. Peronne Marie Thibert, B.H.M. *The Classics of Western Spirituality*. N.Y.: Paulist Press, 1988.

Francis of Assisi. *The Little Flowers of St. Francis*. Trans. Raphael Brown. Garden City, NY: Doubleday, 1958.

Bibliography

Gertrude the Great. *www.my.homewithgod.com/gertrude/book2*

Gregory of Nyssa. "Commentary on the Song of Songs. Sermon 12." *Gregory of Nyssa: The Life of Moses*. Trans. Everett Ferguson and Abraham J. Malherbe. Mahwah, N.J: Paulist Press, 1978

Griffin, Emilie. *www.baylor.edu/Christianethics/MysticismStudyGuide1.pdf*

Hadewijch of Antwerp. *Hadewijch-the Complete Work*. Trans. Mother Columba Hart, O.S. B. Mahwah, NJ: Paulist Press, 1980.

Hildegard of Bingen. *Creation and Christ. The Wisdom of Hildegard of Bingen.* Mother Trans. Mother Columba Hart and Jane Bishop. Mahwah, NJ: Paulist Press, 1996.

Hilton, Walter. *The Scale of Perfection*. abridged and presented by Dom Illytd Trethowan, Trans. Leo Sherley-Price. St. Meinrad, Ind: Abbey Press, 1975.

http://en.wikipedia.org/wiki/Anthony_de_Mello_(priest)

http://en.wikipedia.org/wiki/Joan_Chittister;

http://www.usatoday.com/news/religion/2004-07-20-sister-joan_x.htm

http://www.todayisthatday.com/lawofattraction.html

Ignatius of Loyola. "Letter to Sister Teresa Rejadell." *Letters of St. Ignatius Loyola*. Trans. William J. Young. S.J. Chicago: Loyola University Press, 1959.

Iranaeus, *Adversus Haereses*, Book 4, Chapter 20:7-Fahlbusch, Erwin, Geoffrey W. Bromiley, and David B. Barrett. *Encyclopedia of Christianity*: V. 2. Translated by Geoffrey W. Bromiley. Published by Wm. B. Eerdmans Publishing, 2001. Grand Rapids, Michigan.

John of the Cross. *The Collected Works of St. John of the Cross*. Trans. Kiernan Kavanaugh, O.C.D. and Otilio Rodriguez, O.C.D. Washington D.C. Institute of Carmelite Studies, 1976.

Julian of Norwich. *Revelation of Divine Love*. Trans. Spearing, Elizabeth. London: Penguin Books, 1998

Kowalska, M. Faustina. *Divine Mercy in my Soul: The Diary of the Servant of God Sister M. Faustina Kowalska, Perpetually Professed Member of the Congregation of Sisters of our Lady of Mercy*. Stockbridge, MA: Marian Press, 1987

Le Saux, Henri. *Saccidananda: A Christian Approach to Advaitic Experience*. Revised Edition. Delhi. I.S.P.C.K, 1984.

Lull, Ramon. *The Book of the Lover and Beloved*. Ed. Kenneth Leech, Trans. E. Allison Peers Mahwah, N.J: Paulist Press, 1978.

Madigan, Shawn, C.S.J., ed. *Mystics, Visionaries & Prophets*. Fortress Press: Minneapolis, 1998.

Maximus Confessor. *Maximus Confessor-Selected Writings*. trans. George c. Berthold, intro. Jaraslav Pelikan. Mahwah, NJ.: Paulist Press, 1985.

McGinn, Bernard. www.baylor.edu/Christianethics/MysticismStudyGuide1.pdf

Mechtild of Magdeberg. *The Revelations of Mechtild of Magdeburg: The Flowing Light of God*. Trans. Lucy Menzies. London: Longmans, Green & Co, 1953 .

Meister Eckhart. *Everything As Divine: The Wisdom of Meister Eckhart*. Trans. Edmund Colledge, and Bernard McGinn. Mahwah, N.J: Paulist Press, 1996.

Merton, Thomas. "The Inner Experience: Kinds of Contemplation IV." *Cistercian Studies* VIII, 4, 1983.

Merton, Thomas. *The Wisdom of the Desert*. Boston: Shambala Publications, 2004.

Mother Teresa. *Mother Teresa. Meditations from a Simple Path*. Compiled by Lucinda Varday.N.Y: Ballantine Books, a division of Random House, Inc.,1996.

mystic.Dictionary.com.WordNet 3.0, Princeton University, 2006.

mysticism.Dictionary.com. The American Heritage Dictionary

New Revised Standard Version Bible: Catholic Edition, copyright 1989. Division of Christian Education of the National Council of the Churches of Christ in the United States of America.

Nouwen, Henri J.M. *The Wounded Healer*. Garden City, N.Y.: Doubleday & Company, Inc., 1972.

Petroff, Elizabeth, Ed. *Medieval Women's Visionary Literature*. NY: Oxford University Press, 1986.

Pseudo-MaCarius. *Fifty Spiritual Homilies of St. Macarius the Great*. Trans. A.J. Mason. Willits, CA: Eastern Orthodox Books, 1974.

Rahner, Karl. "God of my Life." *The Practice of Faith: A Handbook of Contemporary Spirituality*. Trans. James M. Demske, S.J. Westminister, MD: Newman, 1966.

Rolle, Richard. *Richard Rolle: The English Writings (Classics of Western Spirituality series)* by Richard; trans., ed. and intro. by Rosamund S. Allen; preface by Valerie M. Lagorio Rolle. Mahwah, N.J. Paulist Press, 1988.

Ruuesbroec, John. *John Ruusbroec: The Spiritual Espousals and Other Works*. Trans. James A. Wiseman, O.S.B. Mahwah, N.J: Paulist Press, 1985. (Part Three: Union Without Difference, B. These Three Unions as the Fulfillment of Christ's Prayer)

Scott, Elizabeth. http://stress.about.com/od/positiveattitude/ht/attraction.htm

Silesius, Angelus. *Angelus Silesius: The Cherubinic Wanderer*. Trans. Maria Shrady. Mahwah, NJ: Paulist Press, 1986.

Soltes, Ori. *Mysticism in Judaism, Christianity, and Islam: Searching for Oneness*. Lanham, MD: Rowman & Littlefield Publ, 2008.

Symeon the New Theologian. *Hymns of Divine Love by Symeon the New Theologian*. Trans. George A. Maloney, S.J. Danville, NJ: Dimension books, 1976.

Tauler, Johannes. *Johannes Tauler: Sermons*. Trans. Maria Shrady. Mahwah, NJ: Paulist Press, 1985.

Teilhard de Chardin, Pierre. "The Mystical Milieu." *Writings in Time of War*. Trans. Rene Hague. San Francisco: Harper & Row, 1968.

Teresa of Avila. "The Book of Her Life." *The Collected Works of St. Teresa of Avila I*. Trans. Kierners Kavanaugh, O.C.D. and Otilio Rodriguez, O.C.D. Washington D.C. Institute of Carmelite Studies, 1976.

Therese of Lisieux. *Story of a Soul: The Autobiography of St. Therese of Lisieux*. Trans. John Clark, O.C.D. Washington DC: Institute of Carmelite Studies, 1976.

Thomas A' Kempis. *My Imitation of Christ*.Trans. Msgr. John J. Gorman Brooklyn, NY: Confraternity of the Precious Blood, 1982.

Thomas, T.K. *The Prayer of the Frog Called into Question*, (April 1999) at (www.findarticles.com/p/articles/mi_m2065/is_2_51/ai_56063940/print)   the Ecumenical Review

Urs von Balthasar, Hans. *Origen-Spirit and Fire: A Thematic Study of His Writings*. trans. Robert J. Daly, S.J. Washington D.C.: The Catholic University of America Press, 1984.www.baylor.edu/Christianethics/MysticismStudyGuide1.pdf, p2.

Vatican/va/roman_curia/congregations//cfaith/documents/rc_con_cfaith_doc_19980624_d emello_en.html

Weil, Simone. "A Letter for Father J.M. Perrin, May 15, 1942 by Simone Weil. God In His Mercy." *Parabola*.Vol.33 Number 2, Summer 2008. N.Y. Society for the Study of Myth and Tradition, Inc., a not-for-profit organization.

Bibliography

William of St. Thierry. *The Golden Epistle.* Trans. Theodore Berkeley, O.C.S.O. Kalamazoo, MI: Cistercian Publ. Inc., 1971.

INDEX

About the Author

Ramona Harris is an adjunct college counselor at Modesto Jr. College, a faculty member of the School of Ministry for the Catholic Diocese of Stockton, a lecturer, and a spiritual director. She is a member of the Spiritual Directors' International organization. Ramona has a Master of Pastoral Studies degree, with a focus on Christian Spirituality; and a Master of Arts degree in Education, School Counseling specialization. As a social worker, probation officer and public welfare manager, Ramona has spent several years employed in the area of human services. She resides in northern California, where she enjoys having the time to pursue her dreams.

Breinigsville, PA USA
24 September 2010

245979BV00002B/1/P